total

BOOKS BY AISHA SASHA JOHN

The Shining Material (2011)

THOU (2014)

I have to live. (2017)

*TO STAND AT THE PRECIPICE ALONE AND
REPEAT WHAT IS WHISPERED* (2021)

total

poems

aisha sasha john

McClelland & Stewart

McClelland & Stewart and colophon are registered trademarks of Penguin Random House Canada Limited.

Published simultaneously in the United States of America.

The authorized representative in the EU for product safety and compliance is Penguin Random House Ireland, Morrison Chambers, 32 Nassau Street, Dublin D02 YH68, Ireland. https://eu-contact.penguin.ie

Library and Archives Canada Cataloguing in Publication is available upon request.

ISBN: 978-0-7710-2485-6
Ebook ISBN: 978-0-7710-2078-0

Cover design by Dylan Browne
Cover image: stockfotocz / Getty
Typeset in Arno by Sean Tai

Printed in Canada

McClelland & Stewart,
a division of Penguin Random House Canada Limited,
320 Front Street West, Suite 1400
Toronto Ontario, M5V 3B6, Canada
penguinrandomhouse.ca

1 2 3 4 5   29 28 27 26 25

Penguin
Random House
McCLELLAND & STEWART

CONTENTS

And everywhere where hope and continuity act
together in reply to the moral evocation of the human
will, a miracle takes place.

From LETTER XVII: THE STAR in *Meditations on the Tarot*
—Anonymous

total

WOLF/
NEST/
PEACE
OF MEET

TOTAL

AS IN, MY/OUR VALUE IS, THANKS

"THE END"

"CONTINUANCE SYNONYM"

THE SPACE WHERE FACTS COMPLICATE KNOWING?

REALITY BEYOND ONE'S CAPACITY TO METABOLIZE IT?

WOULD LOOK AT THE MOON IF I GAVE A SHIT

A WOMAN TEXTS ME ITS PICTURE

IT IS WARM INSIDE AND BEAUTIFUL OUTSIDE

(I AM INSIDE)

IT'S OKAY

IT'S FINE

I DO NOT REMEMBER MY LIFE OR HABITS

I AM NEW TO EVENINGS

MY CO-WORKER HANDS ME A BOOK OF POEMS

MY FRIEND WROTE THE BOOK

PLUS YOU'RE NOT ALLOWED PHYSICAL CONTACT

NO TALKING FOR TEN DAYS AND THERE'S ALSO NO
DINNER

THE HURRICANE VS. MY MOTHER'S COUNTRY

TO LAY IN BED AND HAVE SOUP

BROUGHT TO ME AND ALSO

A COMMUNITY

INTELLECTUAL INTIMACY WITH ELDERS

ONTARIO STRAWBERRIES

ROOM ADEQUATELY AISHA'D

ON SHOULD I LEAVE THE HOUSE

37 ON SATURDAY

WHEN I AM ABLE TO REST, I FEEL THEM REJOICING

SOURCES OF REFUGE

MY BENEFACTORS

THE RECOVERING

EVERY CONVERSATION IS AN OPPORTUNITY TO PRACTISE

WHY ARE PEOPLE SO FUCKING STUPID?

(PHOTO OF MY LEFT HAND STIFFLY BLOCKING THE SUN)

(PHOTO OF M. TWISTING UP FROM THE GRASS)

(NEON YELLOW HOODIE HANGING FROM THAT
CHAIR WHOSE WOVEN LEATHER SEAT IS DRY AS WOOD)

I WANT TO START A SCHOOL FOR BLACK GIRLS

(THE CRINKLED SOLE OF MY LEFT FOOT)

(ARCHIVAL PHOTOS OF VARIOUS WOMEN AND GIRLS
IN THE BLACK PANTHER PARTY)

HALF BARE TREE AT BLUE HOUR

BREATHING HEAVING

BETWEEN DOG AND WOLF

IS GROW IMPROVE?

THAT THE SENSUAL IMPERATIVE OF EMOTION

IS EXPRESSION

WE HAVE BEEN INVITED TO BELIEVE WHAT WE KNOW

IS HE COMPETENT, I.E., NECESSARY?

IS SHE NECESSARY, I.E., IRRESISTIBLE?

A KIND OF DOOR IS GLEAMING OVER HER CHEST.

"I AM ACTIVITY, SEDUCTION, PLEASURE."

ENJOY / UPDATE / AROUSE

THE EARTH AT THE BOTTOM OF THE WATER

SECRET VS. SILENT TEACHER

THE HERMIT VS. HANNAH WEINER

WHY DO YOU PRAY?

IS THERE A SYNONYM CLOSER TO COMPASSION THAN
PATIENCE?

A PERSON WHO LOVES BEAUTY MORE THAN THEY FEAR IT

THE CLOSEST TO NOTHING YOU CAN DO FOR MONEY

TO TOUCH TIME TO ITSELF

RAVE TONIGHT TOMORROW

PERFORMING VS. EMANATING

UNMOORED TO OVERWHELMED

SUCKS AND IS BORING

BIOGEL FULL SET

LOVE U AND SO PROUD

STUDENT: IT'S HARD TO SIT WITH ALL OF THIS PAIN

VALERIE FORSTMAN ROSHI: IT'S HARDER NOT TO SIT

BEGUILING

STICK BY

OR EMBRACE

A SIT, A SHOWER, WALK, CHERUB

PROFESSIONAL EMBROIDERY MACHINE AND A
MARKETING / SOCIAL MEDIA MANAGER

AND OF NEGLECT, ATTEND

THAT THE OPPOSITE OF ABANDON IS CHERISH

I am new
to evenings.

HOW DID A NUB OF GINGER END UP IN THE BED?

ANSWER:

THE CAT

WHEN I SAID I HAVE TO BE FIBROUS SO AS NOT TO BE
CONSUMED I WAS NOT

EVEN FUCKING KIDDING

FYI I AM BLEEDING FROM MY PUSSY

DIVA CAT

KEFIR-CRAZY CAT

TO THE ROAD, THE ROAR

EVERYTHING URGENT, ARGH

401 RICHMOND UGH

FIGURED OUT WHAT A GALLERY IS / DOES

THEY ARE LIKE CHURCHES WHERE ONE CAN PURCHASE
THE FURNITURE

DOES THE CAT FRIED EGG UNDERSTAND ME AS A LARGE
COCONUT-SMELLING CAT?

FROM WHICH COULD TO IS

FROM NOT TO FINE

NEXT TO ALREADY

SKY TO GROUND

REALITY'S REGARDLESS

FROM WHICH COULD TO IS

WOULD LIKE TO WHAT

TRANSPARENT TO UNCOVERED

VIA TUMBLR TO TELEPATHY

SHAME TO EMBARASSMENT

LARGE HANDS TO LARGE FEET

FROM SCRATCHING TO SWOLLEN

CONCERNED TO CALLOUSED

OKAY TO ACCRA

ALMOST TO OBSOLETE

FROM AIIGHT TO LIKE

ANNOYED TO ANGRY

THE LITTLEST ME I HOUSE CRYING

WORLD-FILLED WATER

ONE OUT OF ONE OUT OF ONE OUT OF

THREE

FROM CURIOUS TO KEEN

NOURISHED ON A BLACK GRASS

TENDED BY A DREAM

ISLAND WITH FRESH FIGS AND FLOSS

WELCOME TO IS.

I AM THE AISHA OF IS.

LAST NIGHT I INVENTED JAZZ

THICK

NATURAL AND BOUNCY

SOFT AND NATURAL

BLEEDING

THE SOMETHING I SMELL SMELLING LIKE BLOOD

I'LL NEED TO TELL YOU ABOUT THIS CAT

DREAM IN WHICH COVERING ONE'S ENTIRE BODY IN
TURMERIC CONSTITUTES CHAKRA ZERO

CHAKRA 8 ALSO

BETWEEN SKIN AND SWEATER

CUTE AS A COTTON SWAB

AND WHEN I TAKE MY OMEGA-3S I DON'T CRAVE CHEESE

NOW THAT I'M NOT ANXIOUS ALL THE TIME I CAN
TELL WHEN I'M ANXIOUS

FAITH, HE SAYS

Is experienced as a gestational event in Pisces.
For example, the dream in which there's so much thick oily pasta
Falling into a platter the length of a sidewalk
And I wasn't allowed to eat it
Even though I walked the whole length of the festival
And had to see the pasta flowing

At the end of the dream:
My mom and her friends in semi see-through clothing
Thin they were very
And chic
At the tail of the parade that was them there
I believe they got to eat the pasta but not me

Not me standing up and falling
Drinking coffee and crying
Walking to the place where they sell beer on holidays
And purchasing one called "July"
Because when I cry I am able enough not
To seek anything better than the bad I feel
A song animates what's stale and shrivelled in me
So I have in place of false fraternity an infinite
Impermanent something

They got to eat the pasta but not me:
My problem, my wealth
The hardness, an ocean, the cat
Wants to go outside and I want to go outside too

(It is singular
Eternal
Fleeting
The ache that keeps swirling up and stiffening and then
Softening and stiffening and then—

HOW TO EXPLAIN TO THE CAT'S CLAWS
THAT BENEATH MY SOFT PANTS I HAVE SKIN?

WHEN PEOPLE ARE FUNNY, INDEPENDENT, LISTEN

UNWILLING, DISORGANIZED, RESENTFUL

NIGHTTIME, BEING IN BED, SLEEPING

WHAT ANYTHING MEANS (WHY?)

WHAT I DID RIGHT, WRONG

(WHAT?)

ONE OUT OF ONE OUT OF THREE

THE CAT JUST CLIMBED ATOP ME

I COULD LEAVE MY LAIR TO FIND A WAY

AND QUIT THIS TOWN BECAUSE IT'S FLAT

(I FILL IT WITH MY SOFT HAIR BOUNCING)

THE BETTER AND THE BAD

THE BORING AND THEM'S BUTTS

WHAT FAITH LOOKS LIKE ON A GIRL

TIDY AND UNLINED / TO BELIEVE LOVE

AWAITING-INSTRUCTION AWAKE

I WAS FASTING FROM EVERYTHING AND IT WAS BORING

AND IT SUCKED

THE SPIRITS
IN THE
CORNER
AND THE CAT

THE PLACE ELEGANCE ARGUES GRACE

SOMEONE PUT A SMALL SQUARE OF BLACK FABRIC
ON THE DEAD POSSUM LAYING ON THE CURB
SOUTH ON BROCK STREET

SPOTLIGHT, SHADE

THAT I AM A BAT AND I CAVE

THE LUMINARIES

YELLOW FLOWERS

DAY OF REST AND WEEK

CAT VS. LAMB

BLOOD RED MEN'S T-SHIRT BACKWARDS

WAR WITH WHAT'S RAVENOUS IN ME

I AM NOT HOW I HAVE BEEN INSATIABLE

EATING FAST IS LIKE TAKING DRUGS

BREAD OR SOMETHING I HAVE TO COOK

DISCOVER THE VERSATILITY OF TEMPEH—NO

IMAGINATION INJURY

IMAGINATION AMELIORATION

IMAGINATION REPAIR

FOUR RAISINS

FOUR RAISINS WILL LAST AS LONG AS A BOX IF YOU
EAT THEM AS A PRAYER

HE RECOMMENDS MINDFUL SMOKING

OKAY I JUST FIGURED OUT WHAT JESUS IS A METAPHOR FOR

DID YOU HEAR THE ONE ABOUT THE SUFI SAINT?

RABIA OF BASRA:

"ONE DAY, SHE WAS SEEN RUNNING THROUGH THE STREETS OF BASRA CARRYING A POT OF FIRE IN ONE HAND AND A BUCKET OF WATER IN THE OTHER. WHEN ASKED WHAT SHE WAS DOING, SHE SAID, 'I WANT TO PUT OUT THE FIRES OF HELL AND BURN DOWN THE REWARDS OF PARADISE. THEY BLOCK THE WAY TO ALLAH. I DO NOT WANT TO WORSHIP FROM FEAR OF PUNISHMENT OR FOR THE PROMISE OF REWARD, BUT SIMPLY FOR THE LOVE OF ALLAH.'"

TERRIBLE, MOREOVER, AND LIGHT

IMMEDIATE, CLOSE, PROXIMAL, HERE

THE BRIM

THE VERGE

VS.

A MOUTH, A SPINE, AND A SEX

THE GREAT GIVING UP

A CRY-IN

CLASS PICTURE AND CRY

CROSS-COMMUNITY CRYING

CANADIAN APARTHEID

THIS COUNTRY IS SICK AMIRITE?

DREAM OF BELLY BUTTON BETWEEN MY BREASTS
CLOAKED IN LABIA

THAT MY RAGE MODELS HAVE BEEN MALE RAPPERS

FROM HEARING TO HEEDING

DEAR GOD: WHO AM ME?

THE CAT JUST UPCHUCKED AND RE-ATE HER
CHICKEN TREAT

TO SWALLOW WHOLE AND SQUEEZE SOFT

THE SNAKEHOOD, THE PRIESTESS, THE SUPPLICANT, GOD

THAT YOU WERE NEVER BORN AND WILL NEVER DIE

FROM PERCEIVE TO PREDICT

THE TIME TO QUIT AND BE QUIET

INSIDE, ALONE, OKAY

AND DID NEITHER CARE NOR LIKE

ABOUT WHAT I COULD NOT KNOW NOR NEEDN'T

I SAID TO THE CAT GET AWAY FROM MY BREAD!

GET AWAY FROM MY BUTTER, I SAID

(TO THE CAT)

I am "selfish" and I am rich.

I'M READING THE CARDS THAT GOT LEFT ON THE BED
WHEN I TOOK THE DECK TO THE WINDOW

Us, fucking, all night
In the room beside the kitchen
Where the dog went

The next morning barking
So we climbed out the window
I mean,

Whatever.
I hate people saying the right answer out loud
So you can hear them saying the right answer

So what I don't care
Do you know how much work I have on my life of my line?
And then I have to give something?

GIVE ME WHAT I WANT AND
DO WHAT I SAY
(YOU LITTLE BITCH)

Sex: let loose
Time: control
Body: control

Dance: let loose

Stretch: let loose
Money: control
Let loose: let loose

Control: control

AT FRIEND'S HOUSE

They have a dining room table that doubles as a toilet. There's a lever on the table that opens a hatch in the bench below so that you can pee and then another lever on the table lets you flush. I pee at the table with a rounder androgynous person with an Aquarius sun— (the host is someone else). I'm exclaiming about how weird and open it is and I ask if they shit that way too and yes, in the mornings. What about your periods? It's an otherwise very nice apartment.

Before that running away from confusing apocalyptic situation with a friend who is a Black version of M. We're in a foreign country and no one can really see us—we're a type of ghost. Only other ghosts can see us except fewer people can see M.—only other skinny mixed people. We go into a mall and get weaves. Hers is red. Mine is strange: cornrows with extensions in the form of a bob. I can't tell if it's good or—it's weird. Mostly I feel slighted/resentful but there's a hint of the sense of not being able to bear the Black uniqueness of this hairstyle? And/or a resistance to turn away from comparing myself to M.? Because assessing whether or not I liked the hairstyle would require regarding myself. As central/center. And I wouldn't be able to consider myself in terms of my own singular, materially African divinity *and* in terms of what's considered valuable generally *at the same time* and I'm afraid to lose/manage a kind of sovereignty.

L. saves my life. I am very tall and in the road and she hands me huge sticks so I don't impale myself on the bus? Later, I fall into a job but say no because I have to grieve and she pretends to understand but takes all my vitamins away angrily and the newspaper I'm reading.

IF ONE OF US IS BAD, THEN THE OTHER ONE IS STUPID.

The sky is mauve, cotton, orange, mellow.

NOW, THE CAT

Could if awake hear the long one (me)
Pound into the machine
With her slim and fanning paws

And later say to itself
She's peeing in a cookie tin
In the moonlit night?

And then leaving to the park I love by myself
In the sand scrubbing my fingers through the damp sand
Lifting the sand

I thought I could hold in my beliefs
By not speaking them
And ended up saying oh

There is history
Aloud
And speaking of the history

THE TEMP

The dark, the dawn, the blast
The fall, the black
The baby blue

My thin, sloping-shouldered crush's
Brand new heavy goatee
His eyes allegorical, Obama-esque

When to a long and dangerous pause
An infant colics.
Happy book release!

Happy book release.
A phone rings three times:
"Security."

YOU'VE CALLED FAITH "GOD" AND DOUBT "THE DEVIL"

I'M IN THIS ACADEMY OF SORTS (THINK X-MEN)

and I keep visiting my friends' class and hanging out there.
There's this jewelry that I make, very small and fine
by pouring a shiny metal liquid into the ground—anyway
I'm entertaining my friends before their class and also
inside the class itself and then their teacher
my (YouTube) astrologer, Adam Elenbaas
starts to explain or rather he asks my friend, a top student
to elaborate upon how what I'm doing constitutes "funny magic"
so my friend begins to describe how I fit the model: I do this
thing, this thing that disarms and then I do this other thing:
some sort of effortless spontaneous clowning, and it's successful
in some way, like, it's charming and so I'm sitting there thinking
I'm being celebrated and it feels great and I'm getting jacked and
then out of nowhere Adam switches it and he's like Yeah
so you do *that* (his eyebrows raising in a gesture of, like, cringe)
and then goes on to say something about there needing to be rest
this non-stop movement is exhausting for others too: that I
shouldn't be there, at their class *every day*—and he makes
some sort of signal with his hands and it all resonates so
much as to pierce me: this energy, this anxious, essentially
avoidant energy that articulates itself as gregariousness but
that would be better released in quiet, in repose, in *meditation.*

**IF INSTEAD OF ACQUIRING THE OBJECT TO WHICH
SHE FEELS ENTITLED, SHE INSTEAD DISSOLVES
THE FORCES THAT ARTICULATE THEMSELVES AS
ENTITLEMENT**

SOUL

ROOT INCHES

ALLIGATOR AND OWL

STARED AT ON THE SUBWAY

IS THERE SOMETHING I DON'T KNOW BECAUSE I'M ...
UNINFORMED?

PEANUT BUTTER AND BLACK GRAPES

YELLOW HANGING FLOWERS

NONDUAL MINDFULNESS

A BLAZE IN THE VALLEY

COLOURS OF IRON AND RUST

THOUGHT AS (MERELY) MENTAL SENSATION

NEAR-EMPTY PARK AND I

TIRZAH IN THE PARK AND TEXTING

THE WIND ROARED AS DIRECTION

A SHEPHERD ESSENTIALLY

IRMA VEP

MAGGIE CHEUNG

MORNING MILDLY HORNY

SYLVIA WYNTER RETURN

ADEQUATE SALT

THE INFLUENCE OF AROUSAL

THAT WHICH KEEPS YOUR POWER SECRET FROM ITSELF

THE FAT OF MY AUNTIE'S ARMS

ON LUCK

OCEAN OF PRIOR CAUSES

OPPORTUNITIES TO EAT MAYONNAISE

WHY I ASKED WHAT AN ARROW'S OPPOSITE IS

LAVISH ABSENCE'S ARRIVAL

BABY'S FIRST BLENDER

INAUGURAL SMOOTHIE

STUDFINDER

SPELLING CEILING

IF THERE WERE SUN I WOULD MAKE MYSELF BLACK BY IT

THE PRAYER OF DAWN

IN CYCLES AND CIRCLES

PRODDING 40

WHERE IS LINH LU?

SHE WAS MY FRIEND.

WHEN I SCRUB MY FACE AT NIGHT I FEEL GOLD INSIDE

I HAVE ALL TIME WHEN COVERED IN ARGAN OIL

I MEAN ART COUNCIL

I CAN'T BELIEVE THE GOVERNMENT IS GOING TO MAKE
ME CRAWL OUT OF MY INTESTINES TO EXPLAIN THE
STUFF GOD PUT THERE

AS WELL AS OF COURSE EMBARRASSED TO BE EMBARRASSED

THE LADY AT THE HEALTH FOOD STORE TOLD ME WHEN
I ASKED FOR BERGAMOT OIL THAT BERGAMOT OIL IS
GOOD FOR DEPRESSION DUE TO ANGER AND I WAS
EMBARRASSED TO BE THOUGHT CAPABLE OF
DEPRESSION DUE TO ANGER, DEPRESSION, OR ANGER

WHAT THE FUCK DO PEOPLE DO IN THE EVENINGS
THOUGH SERIOUSLY?

THIRD ZOOM

BLUE ANGORA BERET

SILK KNIT SLEEP

CURATIVE NAP

I AM BEAUTIFUL, MADE QUEEN

SPOTLIGHT ON FLOOR CUSHION

STRESSED SOUNDING SNORE

EVENING CHOCOLATE

SPIT FIRE, FLY

SYNONYM FOR SNOB

VERY SWEET PORRIDGE TO SURVIVE

RITUAL LOSTNESS

I HAD NOT THE HOPE TO WISH

BLACK HOLE BED

HOW I HAVE BEEN NIGGER

HEY WHAT DO YOU GUYS DO WITH YOUR THOUGHTS?

TO FEED TO SANCTIFY TO KNEEL

Chance fertility talent
Well I am going on a learning diet
If not fast

Integrate metabolize sleep
Reception inspiration song
Because in the case that I cannot love

I can yet gnash and
Weep.
"We are dancing the energy of shape

As a function of feeling"—me
I wrote that
On a large piece of washi paper

To cover the hole the boot made
In the wall
When I threw it.

All love is love of
God—
Surprise!

But then I
thought what is
wildness, or
what *worth* is
wildness,
without the
structure of
devotion.

IT MADE SENSE THAT I LOVED YOU BECAUSE

I loved you. That's why it made sense.
You have to love me *more*.
You have to love me for my life
As it is for my life as I am
And seek and find and
Look again at me with softness
And feeling, feeling for my life.
I can be okay in the world and alive
With you hating or raging or made sicker
By the occasion of our love
For the occasion is not the cause.

RECOVERY

I wanted to please you
So that you would be happy
And then I would be happy

Too
Instant noodle night
Black mother havers

Raze
Master yielder
8 hours editing

The reckoning
Do fish bleed?
Do f-f-fishes have blood?

ASSHOLE, EYES

SPINE, THE FLOOR

MY PARENTS' PARENTS' PARENTS' PARENTS

OUR LOVE IS ALL WE AREA

POWER REALITY

PROPHET VS. PIECE OF SHIT

DO YOU BELIEVE IN EXPLANATION?

THE BIG TIDDY CLUB

THE FUCK OF IT

THE GROUNDS ON WHICH THEY BELIEVE THEMSELVES
ENTITLED TO MY ATTENTION

THE INFORMATION IN INJURY

THE ONE WITH VIOLETS IN HER LAP

THE SOMETHING I HAD TO TELL YOU, TOLD

THE SOUND OF A PORCUPINE EATING A PUMPKIN

THERE ARE PEOPLE WHO ARE SO DISGUSTING AND I HAVE
EVEN LET THEM TALK TO ME

TO THE PURE ALL THINGS ARE

TONE

TRANSDIMENSIONAL

WHAT HAPPENS IN BANFF GOES ON THE INTERNET

WHAT IS THE NEPTUNE OF RED?

AS IF I'VE DONE SOMETHING WRONG

AWKWARD, UNPLEASANT, FAKE, UNENGAGED

OH—THAT PRACTICE IS ABOUT FORGETTING

AS WAS, IS

THERE FROM HERE

TO CHOOSE THEN FROM NOW

MY PHILOSOPHY IS STOMACH

MY GOD IS LISTENING

HOW MANY PEOPLE ON EARTH HAVE DISHWASHERS?

HAVE YOU EVER TOLD A STORY IN WHICH YOU WERE
NEITHER GOOD, BAD, WRETCHED NOR CHOSEN?

SOTERIOLOGY

THE TETRALEMMA

LOST UNWANTED COMMUNITY

HALF A KITKAT AND A SLIMY CHICKEN SALAD SAMMY

THE PERCENTAGE OF WHAT I WANT TO COMMUNICATE
THAT CAN ONLY BE PERFORMED

DRINK WATER, TAKE OFF PANTS

YOUR TEARS ON ME, SEEING YOU CRY OR THE FACT THAT
YOU'RE CRYING

THAT EARLY, THIS TIRED

WHAT DEATH IS CHANGE?

CAN YOU HANDLE SOMETHING BEING ITSELF AND NOT
EVERYTHING OR ARE YOU VAIN AND SENTIMENTAL?

MUST, NEED, HAVE TO, WILL

OF MONTHS, I AM NOVEMBER AND DECEMBER

SILENCE AND TALKING

CHAKRA BLUE RATTLE

CLAW SWORD

AND A FRESH PILE OF SOFT SOIL

MY B-B-B-BENEFACTORS

BLOOD HIGHWAY

RISK AND RETREAT

AUDACITY

PRIGGISHNESS

WHETHER I CAN WRITE OFF ROLFING

TO START A BAND STAT

MADE A SALAD ATE A SALAD TIME TO NAP

I HAVE ACCEPTED THAT YOU DO NOT LOVE ME AND THAT
I WILL NOT DIE (FROM THAT)

BAD GUY BEING

SCIENCE OF SELF-SATISFACTION

WHAT IS THE LEAST I CAN GIVE?

ALTERNATELY UNINHIBITED AND SELF-SERIOUS

DENIAL ANTONYM

LET GONE

ARCHANGEL AIRPORT

I WILL NOT LET THEE GO EXCEPT

TIRED

TO OPEN TO WHAT IS ARISING

LENS OF LOVING-KINDNESSS

THE WOUND'S RAVINE

OPEN ENMITY

32 PERCENT TONIGHT

FOUR A.M. ARUGULA

WHAT DO YOU CALL A PROSTITUTE WHO WORKS FOR FREE?

EVERYONE IS RESPONSIBLE FOR THEIR OWN SELF-EXPRESSION

AS IN IT HAS TO BE DONE

AND YOU'RE THE ONE WHO HAS TO DO IT

FROM ALLY TO I-DON'T-KNOW

TENDER, CHERISHING

WARM-HEARTED, BRAVE

~~MESSY, SELF-COMPROMISING, SELF-SHRINKING~~, SAD

~~AVOIDANT, WARRING, DEFENSIVE~~, AFRAID

LAUGH TOGETHER, CRY

WE ACCESS THE MIRACLE

Through ease
Is the hypothesis.
The task is to source from the quiet

Instruction
And from confusion
The instinct organized

As impulse and
Into my arms as extension.
I walk back to the hotel

With two limes and a watermelon.
Tonight:
Water and watermelon

BEFORE I CONTINUE:

Does anyone have a question?
Sorry, *what*?

Kidding shut the fuck up / SHUT UP

AROMATHERAPY IS GOD

NEW NOT-FUCKING-BUCKWHEAT HONEY

IS COURAGE THE RECOGNITION OF NECESSITY?

DRINK WATER, EAT CRACKERS

OKAY AFTER CRYING

DEAR ME (AND EVERYONE)

FROM WITCH TO WISDOM FIGURE

BY GRIEF OR DESIRE

MUSIC AND FORTUNE

STRENGTH AND STUPIDITY

SHOULD I LEAVE MY BEDROOM (TODAY) (AGAIN)

FORGETTING, SAYING FUCK

WHAT IS THE SHAPE OF THE THING THAT I LOST?

AND HOW DOES MY ENTIRE APARTMENT SMELL LIKE
ROSEMARY ESSENTIAL OIL WHEN I PERFORMED NO
ACTIONS TO PRODUCE THIS OUTCOME?

HULLO, IT'S CHRISTMAS

I just learned about light sauce.
Light sauce is oil and salt.
And sometimes they ate that.

I dreamt I couldn't talk.
Ask Auntie about your dream—
Across from the porch

A bush is bouncing. My feet are burning
In the Christmas sun—
Burning, *burning.*

I dreamt that I couldn't speak.

THE FERN

The Brim
The Verge
The Magistrate
Horus
The Lute
Encounters
Caravaggio
The Sage
Ransack
The Loot
Terse
The Frock
Fever
The Range
The Appeasement
The Bereavement
The Last Code
Previous Sin
Waving Wind
The Oak

I made my
Self cry
About something.

"One's personal history, whatever else it is, is a history of one's obedience."

TO HAVE THE DESIRE TO GET MILK AND TO GO
AND GET, ACTUALLY, FROM THE STORE, MILK

In New Balances, running down and then back up six flights
With milk, and to finish the Elenbaas talk about dharma
And the ascendant, and to focus on this question of fountains
So as to begin something, and also to continue
So as to have adequate days to amend, ameliorate, improve, polish
Better that which I've begun—writing, that is—a piece—
About *fountains,* so as to complete an assignment, a "text," for an
Exhibition, so as to get money, so as to give it back (that's right:
TD Visa) so as to negate what was made actual: a meal, an item
A cost, a purchase made mine by my word and will, mindfully or
With the absented head/away daze of being here
Busy and idle, purposed and lost, tasked and unmoored
And owled, as an owl, or with them or one or as yes as one:
Hunting in the night and resting too. Last night I dreamt about a
Group of people and one of them, this man, something
Happened to him. I remembered it so well this morning I imagined
Never being able to forget. So I will, okay, immediately, pop
Into the kitty-cornered grocery store—overpriced, expensive
Windowed, there—and with a wave of my bank card's chip get
Milk.

THE LAST TIME I WAS FLOWERED I GOT CUT

I guess I have to find what is hidden
Pertaining to housekeeping and dance
And that I asked and asked and asked
That I went into the wilderness alone
And both of you were seeing me there
And both of you were watching me
In the wilderness
As a centaur it is painful to be witnessed feeding
Or wanting to eat
Beeswax oozing past an untended edge

I DREAMT

That my home chakra is the 7th
And that there was a woman who was chakra five
And she and her friend lay in a bed
And when I left I saw that they had become sexual
And the reason I could see this is I looked at a film strip in my mind.
She was wearing a white bikini top
And her friend was sucking on her breasts.
Otherwise they seemed entirely platonic as in
When I was around they did
And I received the information in the dream that
The zero chakra was tantamount to rubbing one's body in cadmium
So I googled "cadmium chakra"
And then realized it was turmeric
And googled that
And saw a stock image photo of—covered in turmeric—a beautiful man:
Apprentice monk. Ordination ceremony.
He was very soft-looking and round.
And then Jim sent me a text about the voice memo I sent him
Not working.

I WANT TO SPEND ALL MY TIME ON BEING

A walk
A beer
This book

How I have sanitized or or or
"You're not wrong, and I'm not perfect"
Back in Toronto / Everyone's drunk here

Yolk-coloured sky
Puppet with purple lips
Text message from a Libra

Recovery
Requires moving past the anger of entitlement
From reveal to invent

THE RATE RECEPTION REQUIRES

UM

WILL WATCHING RICKY GERVAIS, JERRY SEINFELD, AND
LOUIS C.K. IGNORE AND INTERRUPT CHRIS ROCK IN
THIS YOUTUBE VIDEO INJURE ME?

RETICENCE FAST

BLACK YES

THAT BY HOLY SPIRIT THEY MEANT BREATH

CHOP WOOD CARRY WATER CONTINUED

MORNING COURAGE

MY SOCKS ON AND GO

ETERNAL AND UNCREATED

NOUNS

ATE PIZZA, GOT HERE AT 2, (HAVE SOMETHING TO TELL YOU)

YOU NEEDN'T WORRY ABOUT IT BEING TOO MUCH

Because nothing true is too much
And anything that isn't true is
Never enough

Pink house, black trim
Mango weed smoothie
Spinning, spinning

I flew to Vancouver *for the day*
To celebrate my mother's 75th birthday and
In the bathroom during brunch

Smoothie.
High, at her hair salon
Wanting to barf

The extra large Blenz hot chocolate
Or go to the hospital
Or get outside.

My dad won't let me
Inside their house and
I'm total

Ly fine.
A year later:
Two 3-foot tubes

Of red light
I find on the street
From which one can smell the sea

Glow upon my 38th birthday
Orchid
Altar

"I do feel something back here. But it doesn't feel like pain. It feels like knowledge."

TO DRINK A WATER AND HAVE SOME KIND OF EVIL DIMINISHED

To be held against a surface willingly
To be fixed to/by an impossibility
To be poured into a vessel so as to exceed it

As an elevator, alligator, stick shift

Or the dark orange of my firmness when I'm just
Entirely loosening, windows shaking
Cuz a person works
From the apartment beside me I can hear the
Sound of a drill

And like the lamb got to school how?
He knew the way
In fact
What Mary's lamb did
Is be undivided from his want entirely
One of the cats finds me curious as I barely look at or regard her

I am wild because I am stupid
And I am stupid because I am wise

THE LIME THE UPSTAIRS APARTMENT RESTAURANTEUR
HANDS ME IS ATTACHED TO A BRANCH

And it is a very small lime.
Something about my bag?
It is the upstairs apartment of a house and junky.
Mel (who's Mel?) comes home. She lives there or something—
whatever.

Then: three kinds of blood pressure testers.
I want the priciest one obviously and
my mom says no: the most basic model for 99 (dollars?).
Each Velcro arm band corresponds to a canonical
Expressionist painting.

Awake my heart beats more quickly than is indicative of optimal health!

Beyond my window the wind blows—to waving—
A soft, little skinny-ass tree.
I am listening to Rick Ross or was.
Future, featured in the song in question,
Tells of a 1000-dollar pair of shoes one might
"Not e'en know" upon.
I'm pretty sure most people would recognize
That his 1000-dollar shoes are a 1000 dollars.
(Okay, actually wait I see his point.)

MY LORD PLEASURE

A CAPPUCCINO AND SOMETHING ELSE

EDAMAME AND A KIND BAR

HOW LITTLE I'VE EATEN TODAY AS A FUNCTION OF
THE THAWED SHRIMP'S STINK

TEENAGE SUBWAY CLAMOUR

SOFT FAT SHINING CHEEKS

WHY THESE PEOPLE THINK THEIR SPECIFIC

NEW UGLY RESTAURANT WILL WORK

6 AMERICAN DOLLARS, THE WIND

FROM WITHHOLD TO RAGE

NOW WHERE IN THE INGROWN HAIR IS MY GOOD PEN

CLIPPED, CALLOUS, UNGRACIOUS, OBLIVIOUS

MISPRONOUNCING, MISPREPRESENTING, ILL-FITTED,
DANDRUFFED

FROM BAD COLD TO BLEEDING

TWO TEAS AND A VEGETABLE BREAKFAST

SO BANKSY IS THE DUDE FROM MASSIVE ATTACK WHO CARES

MY THEORY IS DESIRE

A SITUATION IN WHICH YELLING AND SCREAMING IS
INEVITABLE

ME JUMPING UP AND DOWN

I'VE STOPPED FETISHIZING REVELATORY GUIDANCE

I SWEAT THROUGH THE DARK GREEN TURTLENECK DRESS

THE BABY BLUE CROPPED HOODIE

THE ORANGEY RED T-SHIRT TOO BUT I WORE THAT

ALL DAY ANYWAY

SCISSOROLOGY

MATERIALITY

DAUGHTERHOOD

FLUX

EXCUSE ME WHILE I FUCK THE FIRE

I FEEL SICK AND AND AND NUMB

A PERSON LIKELY TO TEXT ME BACK

MY BIG FLAT BEAUTIFUL FEET

THE MOON

CHILD OF THE SONS OF THE MIGHTY

RULER OF FLUX AND REFLUX

SUPPLENESS

SELF-SATURATED

BIG VS. SMALL (TITTIES)

LOVES BEAUTY, HAS MENTAL PROBLEMS

ON FESTIVITY

MYSTERY SOURCE X TO US

BRITISH ACCENT LESSONS FOR BIRTHDAY

WHO LAUGH AND LIKE ME

THE GREAT NOT-MATTERING

BEFORE OR AFTER FAITH

VIGOUR

LILAC SEASON LAST YEAR

A PERSON UNAFRAID OF HER BEAUTY

INVINCIBLE

MESSY

(FEEL SICK)

AND SCARED AND SMALL

I AM ALLOWED TO FEEL CONFUSED AND SMALL

"WHAT ALCOHOL GOES GOOD WITH (ORANGE)
GATORADE?"

LORENZO IN TAOS OR *WESTWORLD*

CHILI, SUGAR, SALT

THE 8 OF EGGS

WHO IS HERE WHEN I'M ALONE—WHO ARE HERE?

"HER INTELLECT ISSUES IN WISDOM"

IN THE CAVE, IN THE CORNER, UNSEEN

INCREASED CATLIKENESS

AND OBSERVE HOW THEIR BODIES REACT TO WHAT
THEY'RE SAYING

THE BOOK OF

APPETITE AND HUNGER

SOBRIETY AND SATURN

RAY OF GOD

7 YEAR DESERT

THE HARD LIGHT OF THE SUN OR SOFT

TO FIND RIGHT THAT WHICH IS THERE

WHAT'S REAL BY ITS WEIRDNESS

UNKNOWN AND IRIE

WE ENTERED THE VESTIBULE

YOU

WHAT'S THE WORK I NEED TO DO
TO DO THE WORK I NEED TO DO?

ORLÉANS CATHEDRAL AND CRY

THAT I DON'T KNOW ANYTHING AND CAN'T

ACQUIRE STIMULANT, GO OUTSIDE

WHATEVER I WANT FOR AN HOUR

HOW CAN I REMEMBER WHAT I WANT TO FORGET?

EVERYBODY INSIDE ME IS *VACATION*?

I CAN'T BELIEVE OTHER PEOPLE HAVE TO GROW UP AND
LIVE AND THAT I DID ALSO

THE MINIMUM (DO YOU FUCKING LIKE IT?)

BODY BEHAVING?

WHAT IS ITS PROPAGANDA?

THE GREAT LUCK OF LOVING

THE GOOD LUCK OF LOVE

DON'T PREFER

PAIN

(I NEED MEN)

WHERE JESUS MY WHITE HOODIE IS /   OH

I HAVE BEEN INSTRUCTED TOWARDS CRUELTY

THE CAPACITY TO BE IN A SUPPORTIVE RELATIONSHIP
WITH ONE'S VULNERABILITES, OR STRENGTH

MY EMPIRE OF HONESTY

PICTURES OF MY PLANT

WILL I GET TO ANCIENT EGYPT WITH MY EYES OPEN?

DREAMT (LITERALLY) OF A SHIT THAT DID NOT STINK

UNCONDITIONAL ALLOWING

How can there be free will when there's history?

And what do you call
That which transforms
Today into last week?

I WANT TO SPEAK THE SILENCE INTO ITSELF

TO LISTEN AND TALK AT THE SAME TIME

IT WILL BE REVEALED WHERE AND HOW I (DO NOT) FEEL

THAT I AM A PENCIL AND DRAWING

(BUYING CHIPS, EATING MISS VICKIE'S ORIGINAL KETTLE
CHIPS, REMOVING CONTACTS, GREAT LIGHT)

MY BODY FAT PERCENTAGE ALSO

IT WILL BE REVEALED I SPEAK WITH MY SPINE

IT WILL BE REVEALED I AM TRYING TO ENTER MY ARMS
INTO ALL SPACE THEY DON'T OCCUPY

PEOPLE WILL SIMPLY KNOW WHO I AM AND WHAT

INSCRUTABLE, PREGNANT, I KNOW THE PEACE OF THE
DESERT

I KNOW THE SILENCE OF THE DESERT

I KNOW THE PAIN OF THE DESERT

I KNOW THE STRENGTH THAT IS BORNE OF THE DESERT

OUR PRONOUNS ARE WE/US, YOU SAID

HOW, TOMORROW, WILL I KNOW THAT THIS WAS REAL?

MISSING SOMETHING

To sleep when tired / Boredom to experience stillness / Being the
First / To arrive / In order to get to / Where you're meant to be / I
Want you to risk loneliness to learn to pray / To risk singularity /
Beauty: "Anyone in the grips of freedom or pleasure" / Park statue
Of a person giving birth / If iced tea works / Vestibular lilacs / All
Of the earth is my life

ACKNOWLEDGEMENTS

Thank you God/Presence/Being. Thank you, Breath, Time, Water, Body, Rhythm, Fire, Feeling, Order, Laughter, Mystery. Thank you, Grace. Thank you to the Spirits of Dance and Singing. Thank you, Stillness. Thank you, Vastness. Thank you, All.

I would like to acknowledge the funding of the Toronto Arts Council, the Ontario Arts Council, and the Canada Council for the Arts, without which the writing of this book would not have been possible.

Also invaluable to the creation of this work was the time I spent in residency. Blessed thanks to Thread Residency, and to Mamadou Cissé Kanté and Angélique Tine and Mariama Sidibé. Thank you to the Banff Centre for the support of my Leighton Studio Residency. I'm so grateful to have been U of T Scarborough's Writer-in-Residence: hearty thanks to Daniel Scott Tysdal and Andrew Westoll. As I write this, I am Affiliate Artist at Toronto Dance Theatre—loving thanks to Andrew Tay and Rosemary James and the entire TDT staff.

Versions of some of these poems were first published in the following periodicals: *The Capilano Review*, *Feminist Temporalities* (Pelt Vol. 4), *Ex-Puritan*, *Room Magazine*, *Canal*, *Erizo*, *Effects*, NewPoetry.ca, and in the chapbook *TO STAND AT THE PRECIPICE ALONE AND REPEAT WHAT IS WHISPERED* (Ugly Duckling Presse 2021/2), and in *VERSschmuggel / reVERSible: An Anthology of English Canadian Poetry / Poésie du Québec / Dichtung aus Deutschland* (Book*hug 2021).

Important editing of this book happened in the dance studio. Blessed thanks to Devon Snell and Erin Poole for holding the thread with me. And to Nyda Kwasowsky and Ty Temple-Smith.

Thank you to my friends for being sources of inspiration and delight, for seeing me, for praying and laughing and dancing with me, for holding my hand in and through Mystery, for your love: Akemi and GC and Devon and Ellen and Amy and Alexa and Clara and Fan and Charity, thank you.

Thank you to readers of earlier drafts of this work for your feedback and conversation: Fan Wu, Evan Webber, Andrea Actis.

Thank you to my analyst Lindsay Barton for your sacred listening and reframing.

To my mother, thank you for your love and sweetness, and for modelling a singular and savvy version of grace. Thank you for looking at me like I am total.

Thank you to the team at McClelland and Stewart. To Canisia Lubrin, thank you for your keen eye and generosity. For the grace with which you've met me in this. Big thanks to Kelly Joseph, for so much patience and care in the crucial final stages. Thank you Dylan Browne for a stunning cover and all your efforts.

Thank you to Mountain Cloud Zen Center and to teachers Henry Shukman and Valerie Forstman for your practices and teachings of which I have benefited immensely. Thanks to Esther Tishman and the Mindful Tarot community. Thanks to Mala Kline for the imaging work.

NOTES

WE HAVE BEEN INVITED TO BELIEVE WHAT WE KNOW: Italicized lines are from "III L'lmperatrice/The Empress" in *The Way of the Tarot: The Spiritual Teacher in the Cards* by Alejandro Jodorowsky and Marianne Costa, 2009.

HOW DID A NUB OF GINGER END UP IN THE BED?: 401 Richmond is a heritage-designated industrial building in downtown Toronto home to many galleries and artist-run centres.

FAITH, HE SAYS: The "he" is Adam Elenbaas as expressed in *The Sun in Pisces: Faith in the Sign of the Fishes* (YouTube).

THE PLACE ELEGANCE ARGUES GRACE: The references to raisins and mindful smoking are from a Gabor Maté talk on YouTube. The quote about Rabia of Basra is from Wikipedia.org.

TO FEED TO SANCTIFY TO KNEEL: The title, 1st, 4th, and 5th lines are from "XVII L'Etoile/The Star" in *The Way of the Tarot: The Spiritual Teacher in the Cards* by Alejandro Jodorowsky and Marianne Costa, 2009.

THE BIG TIDDY CLUB: "To the pure, all things are pure." Titus 1:15

ALTERNATELY UNINHIBITED AND SELF-SERIOUS: The title of the poem comes from a line in this article: "Matthew McConaughey Wrote the Book on Matthew McConaughey" *New York Times* Oct 14, 2020.

"One's personal history, whatever else it is, is a history of one's obedience.": *Unforbidden Pleasures* by Adam Phillips, 2016.

THE LIME THE UPSTAIRS APARTMENT RESTAURANTEUR HANDS ME IS ATTACHED TO A BRANCH: The song in question is Rocko's "U.O.E.N.O." (feat. Rick Ross, Future).

THE MOON: The first two lines are descriptions of The Moon card in the (Thoth) tarot.

AISHA SASHA JOHN is a performer, choreographer, and poet. She's the author of *I have to live.* (McClelland & Stewart, 2017), a finalist for the Griffin Poetry Prize, *THOU* (Book*hug, 2014), a finalist for the Trillium Book Award for Poetry and the ReLit Poetry Award, *The Shining Material* (Book*hug, 2011), and the chapbook *TO STAND AT A PRECIPICE ALONE AND REPEAT WHAT IS WHISPERED* (Ugly Duckling Presse, 2021). As a dance artist, Aisha is interested in performance as a site of rehearsing being and in the power of reception as creative methodology. She's the inaugural Affiliate Artist at Toronto Dance Theatre where her work *The Pool*, made with the TDT ensemble, will premiere in winter 2025. Aisha's duet *DIANA ROSS DREAM* (Danse-Cité 22), performed with Devon Snell, has been presented in Montreal, Vancouver, and Rouyn-Noranda, and was developed during her 2019-2022 Dancemakers choreographic residency. Aisha's first full-length solo work debuted as *the aisha of oz* at the Whitney Museum in 2017, and in 2018, iterations of *the aisha of is* were presented at Montréal, arts interculturel (MAI) and Toronto's SummerWorks Festival. Winter 2026 will mark the debut of a co-creation with fellow choreographer/performer Clara Furey. Aisha holds an M.F.A. in Creative Writing from the University of Guelph and a B.A. in African Studies and Semiotics from the University of Toronto. She was born in Montreal.